INTIMACY

A Way to Prayer

COPYRIGHT PAGE

INTIMACY: A Way to Prayer

ISBN: 979-8995645-8-9-4

Printed in the United States of America

First Edition

This book is a work of spiritual teaching and reflection. It is not intended to replace personal study, prayer, or the guidance of the Holy Spirit.

DEDICATION

This book is dedicated to the One who first drew near, to God who desired intimacy long before I understood its worth.

To the Holy Spirit, my Teacher, my Companion, my Breath, who patiently led me into the chambers of nearness.

To Jesus Christ, the Word made flesh, whose love opened the way to communion without fear. May every page reflect His heart, His tenderness, and His invitation to dwell.

I also dedicate this work to every believer who has ever longed for more, to the hungry, the weary, the searching, the broken; to those who pray in whispers and those who pray in silence.

May this book become a doorway into the Presence that transforms.

ACKNOWLEDGMENTS

I acknowledge the gentle leadership of the Holy Spirit, without whom this book would not exist. Every revelation, every sentence, and every breath of understanding came from His nearness. I honour the quiet moments when He taught, corrected, comforted, and waited for me.

I acknowledge the Word of God, living and active, which sustained me as I wrote and formed the substance of every chapter.

I am grateful for the unseen cloud of witnesses whose lives testify that intimacy with God is not a theory but a lived reality. I honour every spiritual father and mother whose teachings stirred my hunger for God. And to every reader who will journey through these pages with sincerity, may the same Presence of God rest upon you as you read.

PREFACE

Intimacy is not a subject; it is a calling.

It is not a discipline; it is a relationship.

It is not a technique; it is a posture.

This book was not written from expertise but from hunger. It was not born of study but of encounter. It is the record of a journey into the heart of God, a journey that continues even now. I did not write this book to teach others. I wrote it because God was teaching me. Each chapter became a mirror, revealing where my heart needed to be aligned.

Each revelation became an invitation to draw nearer. Each page became a place where the Holy Spirit whispered, corrected, and breathed life.

This book is not meant to be rushed. It is meant to be received slowly, prayerfully, and with reverence.

My prayer is that as you read, you will encounter not information, but Presence. That you will not simply learn principles, but understand closeness to God. That you will not finish this book as you began it.

Table of Contents

AUTHOR'S NOTE

I approached this manuscript with trembling. Intimacy is holy ground. It is where God reveals Himself, not to the gifted but to the yielded. I am not an intimacy expert; I am a student. I am learning to walk with God, to hear Him, to trust Him, and to surrender to Him. This book is part of that journey. You will find no formulas here. No promises of quick results. No spiritual shortcuts. Intimacy cannot be manufactured; it can only be received. It is the Holy Spirit's work in a willing heart.

I desire that these pages will awaken hunger, not pride; surrender, not striving; nearness, not noise. If at any point you sense the weight of God's presence as you read, pause. Do not rush past it. Let Him speak. Let Him draw you. Let Him work.

This book is not the destination. He is.

INTRODUCTION

There is a place in God where prayer becomes more than words. A place where the heart grows quiet enough to hear Him, where the soul aligns enough to follow Him, and where the believer no longer merely visits God but begins to dwell in Him.

This place is intimacy.

Intimacy is the way to true prayer. It is the environment in which prayer becomes partnership, where the believer no longer prays from earth towards heaven but begins to pray from heaven towards earth. It is the realm in which the will of God becomes the desire of the heart, where obedience becomes joy, and where surrender becomes strength.

This book is an invitation into that reality. It is a journey through the chambers of nearness, from the first stirring of desire to the depth of union.

Each chapter is intentionally crafted to form a pathway to deeper communion. You will encounter the foundations of intimacy, the shaping of the inner life, the cost and reward of closeness, and the maturity of oneness with God.

If you allow the Holy Spirit to guide you, this book will not merely inform you; it will transform you. It will teach you to draw near, to remain, listen, align, and walk with God in the secret place of the heart.

And when intimacy becomes your life, prayer will no longer be something you do.

It will be who you are.

Part One

Foundations of Intimacy

CHAPTER ONE

THE MYSTERY OF INTIMACY

The Question of Nearness

What does it truly mean to draw near to God? Not in language, not in theory, not in religious familiarity, but in lived reality. What does it mean to know Him as a Person rather than merely as doctrine? What does it mean to experience His presence so deeply that your inner life is reordered, your desires purified, and your will gradually align with His?

This is the question that defines intimacy. It separates that content with spiritual activity from those who hunger for nearness. Scripture begins with this question. When God asked Adam, *"Where are you?"* (Genesis 3:9), He was not seeking information; He was revealing distance.

The question was not geographical but relational. It was an invitation to return to proximity.

The psalmist expresses the same longing: *"My soul follows hard after You"* (Psalm 63:8). This is not the language of casual devotion but of pursuit. It is the cry of a heart that refuses distance, a soul that has tasted God and cannot return to ordinary life. Intimacy is not optional; it is essential.

The question is not whether God desires the believer, but whether the believer desires God enough to draw near. *"Draw near to God, and He will draw near to you"* (James 4:8). This is not a suggestion but a response. God meets hunger with Himself.

God does not force intimacy. He invites, stirs, and waits for the heart to respond.

The Hidden Distance

The tragedy of the modern believer is not that God is distant, but that the heart has grown distracted.

Many live on the edge of God's presence. They pray, yet do not commune. They worship, yet do not encounter. They read Scripture, yet do not hear. They know the language of faith, but not its life.

Scripture describes this condition clearly: *"This people draws near to Me with their mouth, and honours Me with their lips, but their heart is far from Me"* (Matthew 15:8). The issue is not expression, but proximity. The lips are near, yet the heart is distant.

Distance from God is not measured in miles but in awareness. A believer may be active in church and yet absent in presence, engaged in ministry and yet barren in secret, confident in speech and yet unfamiliar with His voice.

David understood this longing when he wrote, *"My soul thirsts for God, for the living God"* (Psalm 42:2). He was not thirsty for activity or routine, but for God Himself.

The Crisis of Distraction

The problem is not that believers do not love God. The problem is that their hearts have become crowded. Life fills the soul with noise, responsibilities, anxieties, and ambition. Over time, these accumulate until there is little room left for awareness of God. Jesus warned of this in the parable of the sower, where the cares of life choke what has been planted, rendering it unfruitful (Matthew 13:22).

In this state, prayer becomes a duty rather than a communion. Worship becomes performance rather than posture. Scripture becomes information rather than revelation. Church becomes routine rather than an encounter.

The drift that follows is subtle. It is neither rebellion nor open sin. It is a distance. A quiet, unnoticed distance that gradually becomes normal. It is the kind of distance that feels acceptable because it hides beneath activity.

Martha illustrates this condition. She was not sinful or rebellious; she was simply distracted. Yet Jesus responded, *"One thing is needed"* (Luke 10:42). Distraction, though seemingly harmless, stands in direct opposition to intimacy.

God is not silent, yet the heart is often too loud to hear Him. God is not far, yet the soul is often too preoccupied to notice. God is not hidden, yet life has become scattered. A divided heart cannot sustain intimacy. This is why the psalmist prayed, "*Unite my heart to fear Your name*" (Psalm 86:11).

The Divine Invitation

The solution to distance is not found in greater effort, but in responding to divine invitation. Intimacy does not begin with the believer's pursuit of God, but with God's pursuit of the believer. Jesus revealed this when He said, *"No one can come to Me unless the Father who sent Me draws him"* (John 6:44). The desire to seek God is itself evidence that God is already drawing near.

God is not a distant figure waiting to be discovered; He is a present Father inviting relationship. *"Behold, I stand at the door and knock"* (Revelation 3:20). He does not force entry. He waits for a response.

The Holy Spirit makes intimacy possible. He awakens hunger, softens the heart, and reveals God's nearness. He teaches the believer to recognise God's voice and discern His presence. Without Him, intimacy remains distant; with Him, it becomes accessible.

The Way Back

The answer to spiritual distance is not more activity, but greater awareness. Scripture calls the believer to stillness: *"Be still, and know that I am God"* (Psalm 46:10). Stillness is not passivity but intentional attention. It is the decision to prioritise knowing God above doing for Him.

In stillness, the noise begins to quieten. The heart softens. The soul becomes attentive again. The believer recognises that God has been near all along. God is not found in noise but in the whisper. Elijah discovered this when God revealed Himself not through dramatic manifestations but through a still, small voice (1 Kings 19:12).

The way back is simple, though not always easy. It is a return to stillness, hunger, awareness, and the secret place. It is a return to the simplicity of seeking God for His own sake.

"You will seek Me and find Me when you search for Me with all your heart" (Jeremiah 29:13).

Intimacy is not reserved for the exceptional; it is available to the willing.

Abiding as a Lifestyle

Jesus provides the clearest answer to the question of intimacy when He says, *"Abide in Me, and I in you"* (John 15:4).

Abiding is not striving. It is remaining. It is dwelling. It is choosing to stay. Intimacy is not an event, nor is it a momentary experience. It is a posture of life. It is the continual decision to live in awareness of God's presence.

As the believer yields to this posture, distance dissolves. The noise begins to fade. The heart grows soft. The presence of God becomes tangible. The voice of God becomes clear. Nearness is no longer something visited occasionally; it becomes a place where the believer lives.

The Call to Respond

Intimacy ultimately confronts the believer with a question. Are you living near God, or merely around Him?

This is not a question of activity but of awareness. It is not about how much is done for God, but how much space has been made for Him.

Prayer reveals this truth. It can become a place of routine, predictable and mechanical, or a place of encounter where the soul meets God in sincerity and openness. The secret place is not defined by location but by posture. It is the inward space where the heart turns towards God without distraction.

Life is filled with noise, yet God often speaks in quiet ways. His voice is not forced; it is discernible.

Intimacy requires the willingness to silence external and internal noise to hear Him. The question becomes deeply personal. What would change if space were made for God? What would shift in desire, decision, identity, and direction? What would happen if God were no longer visited occasionally but known continually? Jesus' invitation remains clear: *"Abide in Me, and I in you"* (John 15:4).

Abiding is not temporary; it is a way of life.

Final Invitation

Intimacy begins with a question, but it is sustained by response. God has already taken the first step. The invitation has already been extended. Nearness has already been made available. The question that remains is simple, yet weighty: **Will you come closer?**

CHAPTER TWO

THE ARCHITECTURE OF NEARNESS

The Structure of Proximity

Nearness to God is not a feeling; it is a structure formed within the soul. It is not a momentary experience but a realm the believer learns to inhabit. The question that frames this chapter is simple yet probing: what does it mean to dwell near God, not in imagination or emotion, but in the actual arrangement of the inner life?

Scripture reveals that nearness is not vague; it is patterned. When God instructed Moses to build the tabernacle, He revealed a design of proximity: the outer court, the holy place, and the holy of holies. Each space represented a different degree of access, a different intensity of presence, and a different depth of nearness. God was present everywhere, yet He was not experienced everywhere.

David understood this distinction when he wrote, *"One thing I have desired of the Lord... that I may dwell in the house of the Lord"* (Psalm 27:4). He was not seeking a location, but proximity.

The question of nearness is therefore an architectural one. Where do you dwell in relation to God? Do you live in awareness of Him, sensitivity to Him, or abiding in Him? Jesus made this clear when He said, *"Abide in Me, and I in you"* (John 15:4). Abiding is not visiting. It is not occasional awareness. It is dwelling.

The deeper question is not whether you love God, but whether you live in Him. Where does your heart rest? Where does your mind return? Where does your soul feel at home? These questions reveal the architecture of your nearness.

The Problem of Misunderstood Nearness

Nearness is often assumed rather than understood. Many believe that because God loves them, they are automatically close to Him. Yet love and nearness are not the same. God loved Israel, yet declared, "*This people draws near to Me with their mouth… but their heart is far from Me*" (Isaiah 29:13). Love is God's posture towards man; nearness is man's posture towards God.

One central problem is the assumption. Nearness is often treated as effortless, as though occasional prayer or moments of worship guarantee proximity. But nearness is not measured by emotion or activity; it is measured by habitation. Jesus did not say, "Visit Me," but "Abide in Me."

Another problem is inconsistency. The heart drifts easily, pulled by responsibilities, desires, and distractions. A divided heart cannot sustain nearness. This is why David prayed, "*Unite my heart to fear Your name*" (Psalm

86:11). Without unity of focus, the architecture of nearness begins to collapse.

Misplaced confidence further complicates the issue. Many equate serving God with being near to Him. Yet Martha served while remaining inwardly distant, and Jesus gently revealed that nearness is found not in activity but in attention (Luke 10:41–42). Activity can mimic intimacy, but it cannot replace it.

Emotional dependency also distorts understanding. Some believers feel close to God only when their emotions are heightened. Yet emotions fluctuate, and nearness built on emotion will always be unstable. Scripture instead calls the believer to stillness, where God is known beyond feeling (Psalm 46:10).

At the root of these issues is a lack of structure. Many desire nearness but have never been taught that it has depth, progression, and form. Without this understanding, desire gives way to frustration.

The heart also becomes crowded. The pressures of life, worry, ambition, comparison, and noise fill the inner space meant for God. As Jesus warned, the cares of this world can choke the seed (Matthew 13:22). A crowded heart cannot sustain awareness of God's presence.

Finally, there is misalignment. Many desire God's presence without yielding to His ways. Yet Scripture asks, *"Can two walk together, unless they are agreed?"* (Amos 3:3). Nearness requires alignment. It requires the will to yield and the heart to be shaped.

The Divine Blueprint

The solution to distance is not found in effort alone, but in responding to what God has already initiated.

Nearness begins with God's drawing. Jesus said, *"No one can come to Me unless the Father...*

draws him" (John 6:44). The desire to seek God is itself evidence that God is already at work within the heart.

The Holy Spirit establishes the structure of nearness within the soul. He awakens awareness, restores sensitivity, and leads the believer into truth. His work is not external but internal, shaping the heart to perceive God rightly.

The first movement is awareness. This is the foundation of nearness, the recognition that God is present even when He is not felt. As David wrote, *"Where can I go from Your Spirit?"* (Psalm 139:7).

Awareness shifts the believer from searching for God externally to recognising Him internally.

The second movement is sensitivity. This is the development of perception, the ability to discern God's voice and movement. Elijah discovered that God was not found in dramatic displays, but in a still, small voice (1 Kings 19:12). Sensitivity trains the inner life to recognise that voice.

The third movement is surrender. Here, the believer yields to God's will, aligning the heart with Him. Surrender is not loss, but access. It opens the way into deeper nearness.

The fourth movement is dwelling. This is where nearness becomes a way of life. Jesus' command to abide reveals that intimacy is not occasional but continual. Dwelling transforms nearness from experience into identity.

The fifth movement is alignment. The believer's desires, thoughts, and actions begin to reflect God's heart. Alignment stabilises nearness and prevents drift.

Stillness sustains this structure. It quiets the inner life, creating space for God's presence to become clear. Without stillness, the soul remains too noisy to perceive God.

Consistency sustains it. Nearness is not built in moments but through daily returning. It is the steady practice of remaining aware, responsive, and surrendered.

The Call to Dwelling

Nearness ultimately confronts the believer with a question.

Where do you dwell?

Not where you worship or serve, but where your soul truly lives. Scripture declares, *"He who dwells in the secret place of the Most High shall abide under the shadow of the Almighty"* (Psalm 91:1). Dwelling is not occasional; it is habitual. It is the place the heart returns to without effort.

Is the secret place your home or merely your destination? Do you live there, or do you visit only when life becomes heavy?

What occupies the inner space of your life? Nearness requires room. It requires a heart not filled with competing voices. If the soul is crowded, awareness diminishes.

Another question emerges: do you abide, or do you visit? Abiding is the decision to remain. It is the refusal to drift. It is the quiet, consistent choice to live in God's presence. There is also the question of alignment. Has your life been arranged around God, or is God expected to fit into your life's arrangement? Nearness cannot be sustained without agreement.

Finally, the question deepens: how far do you want to go? Nearness is not static. It is a progression, from awareness to sensitivity, from sensitivity to surrender, and from surrender to dwelling. The invitation is not merely to sense God occasionally, but to live in Him continually.

Final Invitation

Nearness begins with a question, but it is sustained by response. The structure has already been provided. The invitation has already been extended. The presence of God is not distant; it is accessible. The question that remains is simple: **Will you dwell?**

CHAPTER THREE

INTIMACY AS ACCESS

The Question of Access

What does it mean to have access to God? Not access to His blessings, promises, or interventions, but access to Him, His heart, His thoughts, His presence, His inner chambers.

This is the question that defines intimacy as access.

Scripture reveals that not all prayer is offered from the same place. Some pray from a distance, others from nearness. Some pray from the outer court, others from the inner chamber, where God's heart becomes the atmosphere of intercession. The question is not whether God hears prayer; He does. The question is whether the believer is praying from a place of access.

Jesus revealed this when He said, "No longer do I call you servants… but I have called you friends" (John 15:15). Friendship is access. It is the privilege of knowing what others do not know and hearing what others do not hear. It is an invitation into the inner life of God.

Access is not automatic. It is relational. It is the fruit of nearness.

"To you it has been given to know the mysteries of the kingdom of heaven" (Matthew 13:11). Mysteries are not revealed to the distant, but to the close. They are not entrusted to the casual, but to the yielded.

The question, then, is simple: from where do you pray? Do you pray from the edges of God's presence or from within it? Do you pray from information or from revelation?

The Illusion of Proximity

The challenge for many believers is not a lack of desire for God, but a misunderstanding of access. Because God is omnipresent, nearness is often assumed to be automatic. Because God hears all prayers, it is assumed that all prayers carry the same authority. Yet Scripture reveals that proximity and access are not identical.

God's love is universal; access is relational.

Jesus loved all twelve disciples, yet only a few were invited into deeper moments of revelation. This distinction is not about exclusion but about closeness. Access is granted where intimacy is cultivated.

Spiritual casualness further limits access. Many approach God without stillness, without preparation, without alignment. They speak but do not listen. They ask but do not yield.

Yet Scripture asks, *"Who may ascend into the hill of the Lord?"* and answers, *"He who has clean hands and a pure heart"* (Psalm 24:3–4). Access is not casual; it is consecrated.

Another barrier is misplaced identity. Many approach God as servants rather than as sons and daughters. They pray out of duty rather than out of relationship. Yet Jesus made it clear that access flows from a relationship with the Father (John 16:27). When identity is misunderstood, access is limited.

There is also the problem of dulled sensitivity. A distracted, noisy inner life makes it difficult to hear God's voice. Yet God often speaks quietly, as Elijah discovered in the still, small voice (1 Kings 19:12). Access requires the ability to recognise that voice.

Finally, many pray from the wrong place. They pray from anxiety rather than intimacy, from fear rather than faith. They pray towards God as though He were distant, rather than from the awareness of His nearness. True prayer begins with the recognition that the believer stands before the Father.

The Conditions of Access

Access is not earned but is stewarded. It requires a heart prepared to host God's presence.

Purity of heart is essential. This is not perfection but undivided devotion. *"Blessed are the pure in heart, for they shall see God"* (Matthew 5:8). Purity clears the inner life and sharpens spiritual perception.

Consistency in the secret place sustains access. Jesus taught that what is cultivated in secret becomes visible in public (Matthew 6:6). Occasional pursuit cannot sustain continual access. It is formed by daily return, by remaining rather than visiting.

Stillness creates the environment in which access becomes clear. "*Be still, and know that I am God"* (Psalm 46:10). Without stillness, the soul remains too crowded to perceive His presence.

Alignment is equally necessary. "Can two walk together, unless they are agreed?" (Amos

3:3). Access requires agreement with God's heart, ways, and direction.

Where alignment is absent, access is limited.

Faith completes this posture. "Let us... come boldly to the throne of grace" (Hebrews 4:16). Boldness is not arrogance but confidence in the finished work of Christ.

It is the assurance that the door is open.

The Pathway into Access

Access begins with Christ. "I am the door" (John 10:9). He does not merely show the way; He is the way.

The Holy Spirit leads the believer inward. He awakens awareness, restores sensitivity, and guides the heart into deeper alignment with God. His work is not external but internal, forming the capacity for access.

The journey towards access unfolds progressively. It begins with awareness of God's presence, deepens into sensitivity to His voice, moves towards surrender of the will, and matures into abiding.

Abiding is the highest expression of access. Jesus said, "Abide in Me, and I in you" (John 15:4). This is no longer occasional nearness but continual dwelling. It is the life in which the believer does not merely approach God but lives from Him.

In this place, prayer changes. It is no longer directed towards God from a distance, but flows from communion with Him. The believer begins to pray from His heart, aligned with His will and moved by His Spirit.

Access becomes not an experience but a position.

The Call to Enter

Access ultimately confronts the believer with a decision.

From where do you pray? From a distance or from nearness? From fear or from faith? From effort or from union?

The deeper question is this: do you desire access, or do you desire God? Access is not a means to answers, power, or direction. It is the privilege of knowing Him.

What has taken shape within your inner life? Has your heart been shaped to host His presence, or has it been filled with competing concerns? Access requires space. It requires a life arranged around God, rather than God being fitted into the margins of life.

Nearness invites deeper movement. It calls the believer beyond occasional encounters into continual dwelling.

Final Invitation

Access begins with an invitation, but it is sustained by a response.

The door has already been opened, and the pathway has already been prepared. God's presence is not distant, it is available.

The question that remains is this: **Will you enter?**

CHAPTER FOUR

INTIMACY AS SPIRITUAL INTELLIGENCE

The Question of Perception

What does it mean to know God with intelligence? Not the intelligence of the mind, but the intelligence of the spirit, the capacity to perceive God accurately, interpret His movements, understand His voice, and navigate life with the wisdom that flows from communion. What does it mean for intimacy to produce discernment? What does it mean for closeness with God to become the believer's operating system?

Spiritual intelligence is not brilliance, mental sharpness, or theological mastery.

It is the ability to think with God rather than merely think about Him. It is the capacity to see from His perspective rather than through human limitations. It is the ability to interpret reality through revelation rather than through emotion or logic.

Paul prayed that believers would receive "the spirit of wisdom and revelation in the knowledge of Him" (Ephesians 1:17). Revelation unveils God; wisdom applies what has been revealed. Together, they form spiritual intelligence.

The question is not whether God speaks, He does. The question is whether the believer has the capacity to understand Him.

Jesus said, "My sheep hear My voice" (John 10:27). Hearing is intimacy. Understanding is intelligence. Following is obedience.

The deeper question, then, is this: do you know God deeply enough to discern Him clearly?

The Crisis of Spiritual Dullness

The challenge for many believers is not that God is silent, but that they lack the inner capacity to interpret Him.

They hear, but cannot decode. They sense, but cannot translate. They receive impressions, but cannot turn them into direction.

Scripture describes this condition plainly: *"You have become dull of hearing"* (Hebrews 5:11). Dullness is not deafness; it is desensitisation. It results from a distracted and divided inner life. Many rely heavily on natural reasoning, attempting to understand spiritual realities through logic alone. Yet Scripture teaches that spiritual things are spiritually discerned (1 Corinthians 2:14). Logic can assist, but it cannot replace revelation.

Another source of confusion is the multitude of internal voices. Fear, memory, desire, emotion, and cultural influence all compete for attention. Without intimacy, these voices blend with the voice of God, making discernment difficult. As Jesus said, "A stranger they will not follow" (John 10:5). Confusion often reveals distance.

A lack of stillness further weakens perception. God often speaks quietly, not by force but by subtlety. Elijah encountered Him not in the dramatic, but in the still, small voice (1 Kings 19:12). When the inner life is noisy, discernment diminishes.

Immaturity also plays a role. Discernment develops over time. Hebrews teaches that maturity belongs to those who have trained their senses through practice (Hebrews 5:14). It is cultivated, not instant.

Misinterpretation is another barrier. Believers often confuse conviction with condemnation, delay with denial, and silence with absence. These misunderstandings weaken confidence and distort perception.

At the heart of these issues is distance. Spiritual intelligence cannot exist apart from intimacy. The closer the believer is to God, the clearer His voice becomes. Nearness clarifies; distance distorts.

The Formation of Spiritual Intelligence

Spiritual intelligence is not merely learned; it is formed. It is not the result of intellectual effort alone but the fruit of alignment with God.

Jesus said, "He will guide you into all truth" (John 16:13). Guidance is intelligence in motion. Truth is revelation in expression. This formation begins with intimacy. The closer the believer is to God, the sharper their discernment. Daniel was described as having "an excellent spirit" (Daniel 6:3), and that excellence flowed from his relationship with God.

The renewing of the mind is also essential. "Be transformed by the renewing of your mind" (Romans 12:2). A renewed mind becomes capable of hosting divine thought. It shifts from natural reasoning to spiritual understanding.

Scripture provides the foundation. "The entrance of Your words gives light" (Psalm 119:130). Without Scripture, impressions lack grounding and can easily mislead. With Scripture, discernment is anchored.

Stillness sharpens perception. "Be still, and know that I am God" (Psalm 46:10). In stillness, inner noise subsides, and the voice of God grows clearer. It is in quiet that perception deepens.

Practice strengthens discernment. Hebrews teaches that discernment grows through use (Hebrews 5:14). As the believer responds to God, sensitivity increases and clarity develops. The Holy Spirit remains central in this process. *"The Spirit searches all things... the deep things of*

God" (1 Corinthians 2:10). Spiritual intelligence is not self-generated; it is Spirit-formed.

Reverence also shapes perception. *"The fear of the Lord is the beginning of wisdom"* (Proverbs 9:10). Reverence aligns the heart, creating the posture necessary for discernment. Through these processes, the believer moves beyond simply hearing God to understanding Him. They begin not only to walk with God, but to think with Him.

The Call to Discernment

Spiritual intelligence ultimately confronts the believer with a question. What is shaping your perception of God?

Is it noise, fear, distraction, or self-reliance? Or is it intimacy, stillness, and alignment?

Do you desire to hear God, or to understand Him? Hearing may come quickly, but understanding requires surrender, patience, and formation. Are you willing to allow the Holy Spirit to retrain your thinking? Spiritual intelligence is not natural; it is imparted. It requires the renewal of the mind and the transformation of the inner life.

The invitation is deeper than perception; it is participation. It is the call to think with God, to interpret life through His perspective, and to move in alignment with His wisdom.

Final Invitation

Intimacy is not only nearness; it is intelligence.

The mind of Christ is not distant; it is available. Scripture declares, *"We have the mind of Christ"* (1 Corinthians 2:16). The question is whether the believer is aligned enough to receive it.

God is speaking.

God is revealing.

God is guiding.

The question that remains is this: **Will you allow Him to make you spiritually intelligent?**

Part Two

The Formation of the Inner Life

CHAPTER FIVE

INTIMACY AS ALIGNMENT

The Question of Agreement

Alignment is one of the deepest proofs of intimacy, yet it is often the least understood. To walk with God is not merely to love or seek Him; it is to agree with Him. Scripture asks, "Can two walk together unless they are agreed?" (Amos 3:3).

Agreement is not intellectual assent; it is relational synchrony. It is the inward bending of the heart towards the will of God until His desires become the believer's, His rhythms become their rhythms, and His voice becomes their compass.

Jesus revealed the posture of alignment when He prayed, *"Not My will, but Yours be done"* (Luke 22:42).

Alignment is not perfection; it is surrender. It is the decision to yield one's internal compass to God's leadership, to choose His direction over personal impulse, His timing over urgency, and His wisdom over human reasoning.

The deeper question is unavoidable: can intimacy exist without alignment?

Jesus answered this when He said, "If anyone loves Me, he will keep My word" (John 14:23). Love expresses itself in alignment. Without alignment, intimacy becomes emotional and unstable.

Alignment gives intimacy structure.

It transforms affection into obedience, desire into direction, and nearness into partnership.

The question, then, is simple: is your inner life sufficiently aligned for God to walk with you?

The Fractures of Misalignment

The crisis for many believers is not the absence of love for God, but the absence of alignment with Him.

The spirit may reach for God while the will resists Him. Words may express devotion while decisions contradict it. The heart may long for His presence while habits pull it away from His voice. Jesus described this tension: "These people honour Me with their lips, but their heart is far from Me" (Matthew 15:8).

Misalignment often begins with desire. As James writes, "Each one is tempted when he is drawn away by his own desires" (James 1:14). Desire shapes direction. When desire is unformed or divided, the believer drifts, even while remaining outwardly engaged with God.

The will is another point of fracture. Jesus declared, "My food is to do the will of Him who sent Me" (John 4:34). Yet many seek God's blessings while resisting His instructions, creating internal conflict that weakens intimacy.

Priorities also reveal alignment. "Seek first the kingdom of God" (Matthew 6:33). When God is not first, intimacy loses clarity. Competing priorities dilute spiritual focus.

Rhythms of life matter as well. God moves with intention and pattern, yet many live in constant distraction, hurried, fragmented, and inconsistent. Without rhythm, alignment becomes unstable.

Identity is another critical factor. *"You are a chosen generation, a royal priesthood"* (1 Peter 2:9). When identity is unclear, direction becomes uncertain. a believer who does not understand who they are cannot consistently walk in agreement with God.

The mind also plays a role. "Be transformed by the renewing of your mind" (Romans 12:2).

A mind shaped by fear, culture, or past experience cannot sustain a divine perspective.

Finally, affections determine direction. "Where your treasure is, there your heart will be also" (Matthew 6:21). A divided heart cannot sustain alignment.

These fractures, within desire, will, priorities, rhythms, identity, thinking, and affection, create a life that may love God yet struggles to walk with Him.

The Formation of Alignment

Alignment is not achieved by effort alone; it is formed through surrender and sustained by intimacy. It begins with surrender. Jesus' prayer in Gethsemane is foundational: "Not My will, but Yours be done" (Luke 22:42). When the will yields, alignment begins.

The renewing of the mind deepens this alignment. "*We have the mind of Christ*" (1

Corinthians 2:16). Scripture reshapes thought, replacing fear with faith and confusion with clarity. The Word becomes the standard by which life is measured.

Obedience strengthens alignment. "If you love Me, keep My commandments" (John 14:15). Obedience is not a restriction; it is agreement in action. Each act of obedience sharpens alignment and reinforces intimacy.

Intimacy itself sustains alignment. *"Abide in Me, and I in you"* (John 15:4). Nearness brings clarity, and clarity strengthens agreement. Distance breeds confusion; intimacy restores direction.

Desire must be refined. "*Delight yourself in the Lord, and He shall give you the desires of your heart"* (Psalm 37:4). As desire is shaped by God, it begins to reflect His purpose rather than compete with it.

Rhythms of life stabilise alignment. Jesus regularly withdrew to pray (Luke 5:16).

Consistent rhythms create space for alignment to develop and endure.

Identity completes alignment. When the believer understands that they are chosen, set apart, and called, alignment becomes natural rather than forced. Identity anchors obedience and stabilises direction.

Through these processes, intimacy becomes agreement. The believer no longer struggles to align with God and begins to move in step with Him.

The Call to Alignment

Alignment ultimately poses a question to the believer. What part of your life is out of alignment with God?

Is it your desires, priorities, rhythms, thinking, identity, or will?

Alignment begins with honesty. It requires the courage to see clearly and the willingness to change.

Are you willing to allow God to reorder your inner life? Alignment requires surrender and truth. It also requires releasing control and embracing direction.

Do you desire intimacy deep enough to agree with God, even when it costs you? Agreement is not always easy, but it is necessary. Alignment is the pathway through which intimacy becomes functional and enduring.

Final Invitation

Alignment is not forced; it is invited. God is already walking. The question is whether you are sufficiently aligned to walk with Him. Intimacy is not only nearness, but it is also agreement.

Will you allow God to align you so you can walk with Him?

CHAPTER SIX

INTIMACY AS AUTHORITY

The Nature of True Authority

Authority is one of the most sacred inheritances of intimacy, yet it is often misunderstood. Many associate authorities with force, volume, or spiritual aggression, but Scripture reveals a different reality: authority flows from nearness to God.

Jesus declared, *"All authority in heaven and on earth has been given to Me"* (Matthew 28:18), and He entrusted that authority to those who walk with Him. Authority is not seized; it is received. It is the result of a union.

Jesus did not teach His disciples to pursue authority; He taught them to pursue Him. Authority emerged from that relationship.

When the seventy returned rejoicing that demons submitted to them, Jesus redirected their focus: *"Do not rejoice that the spirits submit to you, but rejoice that your names are written in heaven"* (Luke 10:20).

Their authority was rooted in relationship, not performance.

The question, then, is unavoidable: can authority exist without intimacy?

Jesus answers this directly: *"Apart from Me you can do nothing"* (John 15:5). Authority without intimacy becomes imitation. It becomes noise without weight, activity without effect, declaration without impact.

True authority is the overflow of union; a life so aligned with God that it becomes a vessel of His will and an extension of His dominion.

The Failure of Imitated Authority

The crisis for many believers is not the absence of authority, but the absence of the intimacy that sustains it.

They speak, yet nothing shifts. They declare, yet nothing responds. They pray, yet nothing moves.

Scripture offers a sobering example. The sons of Sceva attempted to cast out demons "by Jesus whom Paul preaches," but the spirit replied, "Jesus I know, and Paul I know, but who are you?" (Acts 19:15). Their failure was not in their words, but in their distance. They attempted to wield authority without relationship, and the gap was exposed.

Authority also weakens when it is mistaken for emotional intensity. Elijah called down fire with a simple prayer. Jesus calmed storms with a word.

Authority is not loud; it is grounded. It is the quiet force of a life aligned with God.

Another fracture appears in identity. “As He is, so are we in this world” (1 John 4:17). A believer who does not understand their identity cannot walk in authority. When identity is unstable, authority becomes inconsistent.

Disobedience further undermines authority. “If you love Me, keep My commandments” (John 14:15). Authority is not a badge; it is a trust. It is entrusted to those who walk in alignment with God’s will.

Finally, authority weakens in the absence of spiritual depth. A life disconnected from prayer and the Spirit cannot carry weight. Authority is not sustained by words but by presence.

The Formation of Authority

Authority is restored not by striving but by returning to intimacy, identity, obedience, and presence. It begins with abiding. “Abide in Me, and I in you" (John 15:4). Abiding forms the foundation of authority. When the believer dwells in God, they bear His nature, His presence, and His authority.

Identity strengthens authority. "You are a chosen generation, a royal priesthood" (1 Peter 2:9). Authority is not arrogance; it is awareness, an understanding of who the believer is in Christ.

Obedience sharpens authority. "Why do you call Me 'Lord, Lord,' and do not do what I say?" (Luke 6:46). Authority operates effectively only when it enforces God's will, not personal preference.

Purity gives authority clarity. *"Blessed are the pure in heart, for they shall see God"* (Matthew 5:8). A pure heart carries weight in the spirit. Faith activates authority. *"If you have faith..."* (Matthew 17:20).

Faith does not strive; it stands. It commands from confidence, not from fear.

The Holy Spirit empowers authority. *"You shall receive power when the Holy Spirit has come upon you"* (Acts 1:8). Without the Spirit, authority becomes mechanical; with the Spirit, it becomes supernatural.

Consistency sustains authority. A life that walks with God daily becomes a life that carries authority naturally.

The Call to Dominion

Authority ultimately confronts the believer with a question. Do you desire authority that flows from intimacy, or authority that exists apart from God?

What part of your life resists the intimacy that produces authority? Is it fear, distraction, inconsistency, or unbelief?

Authority begins where identity is restored, and intimacy is cultivated. It is not something added to the believer; it is revealed through their union with God.

Final Invitation

God does not force authority; He invites the believer into it.

Intimacy is not only nearness—it is dominion.

Will you walk closely enough with God for your life to carry His authority?

CHAPTER SEVEN

THE DISCIPLINE OF STILLNESS

The Nature of Stillness

Stillness is one of the most demanding disciplines of intimacy, yet it is essential. In a world defined by noise, movement, and constant stimulation, the soul often forgets how to be quiet before God.

Scripture calls the believer into a posture that is not passive but deeply intentional: “Be still, and know that I am God” (Psalm 46:10). Stillness is not inactivity; it is surrender. It is the quieting of the inner life so the spirit can perceive God clearly.

Stillness is not merely silence; it is the alignment of the inner world.

It is the heart ceasing from striving, the mind from agitation, and the soul learning to rest in God.

Jesus described this rest when He said, "Come to Me… and I will give you rest" (Matthew 11:28). This rest is not escape; it is communion.

The Crisis of Noise

The challenge for many believers is not that God is silent, but that they are too internally loud to hear Him.

The mind races.
The emotions surge.
The soul remains restless.

Isaiah captures this tension: *"In returning and rest you shall be saved; in quietness and confidence shall be your strength. But you would not"* (Isaiah 30:15). The issue is not inability; it is resistance.

Restlessness is the first barrier. The soul becomes conditioned to activity and uncomfortable with stillness. Even in silence, the mind continues to move.

Fear of silence deepens the problem. Stillness exposes what is hidden, wounds, anxieties, and unresolved thoughts. Yet it is often in that exposure that God begins to speak.

The culture of hurry further undermines stillness. Jesus moved with purpose, but never with urgency. He regularly withdrew to pray (Luke 5:16). Modern rhythms, however, often run counter to the Spirit's pace.

Mental noise also disrupts perception. Thoughts multiply and compete for attention. Stillness is not the absence of thought but the ordering of thought in the presence of God.

Spiritual impatience adds another layer. Many expect immediate answers, yet God often works slowly and quietly. Stillness becomes the training ground for patience.

The Formation of Stillness

Stillness is not natural; it is cultivated. It is a discipline that develops through intentional practice. It begins with surrender. "*Truly my soul waits for God*" (Psalm 62:1). Waiting is not passive; it is an act of trust.

Trust deepens stillness. "*In quietness and confidence shall be your strength*" (Isaiah 30:15). Trust quiets fear and steadies the heart.

Scripture anchors the mind. Meditation on the Word replaces internal noise with truth, bringing focus and clarity to the inner life (Joshua 1:8).

The Holy Spirit sustains stillness. "The Spirit Himself bears witness with our spirit" (Romans 8:16).

His voice is not forced; it is perceived. Stillness makes that perception possible.

Peace becomes the atmosphere of stillness. "*My peace I give to you*" (John 14:27). This peace is not the absence of conflict, but the presence of Christ.

Consistency makes stillness a lifestyle. As seen in the lives of Daniel and David, regular rhythms create space for sustained intimacy.

The Call to Quietness

Stillness ultimately poses a question to the believer.

What noise is drowning out the voice of God in your life?

Is it fear, distraction, hurry, or inner unrest?

Are you willing to let God slow you down so you can hear Him clearly?

Stillness requires surrender, trust, and courage. It is not empty, it is receptive. It is the space in which God reveals Himself.

Final Invitation

God is speaking. The question is whether the soul is quiet enough to hear Him.

Stillness is not absence; it is an invitation.

Intimacy is not only nearness, but it is also quietness.

Will you be still enough for God to reveal Himself to you?

CHAPTER EIGHT

THE LANGUAGE OF INTIMACY

The Nature of Divine Communication

Every relationship has its own language, and intimacy with God is no exception. The deeper the intimacy, the clearer the communication.

God is not silent; He is speaking. Scripture affirms this: "*The Lord speaks once, yes twice, yet man perceives it not*" (Job 33:14). The issue is rarely God's silence; it is the believer's sensitivity. Intimacy sharpens that sensitivity until communication becomes internal rather than external, relational rather than occasional.

The question, then, is clear: what is the language of intimacy?

God communicates in many ways through Scripture, His Spirit, impressions, peace, conviction, wisdom, silence, and His dealings. Jesus said, "*My sheep hear My voice... and they follow Me*" (John 10:27).

Hearing is not merely auditory; it is relational. Recognition flows from familiarity and follows from trust.

Jesus deepened this understanding when He said, *"No longer do I call you servants... but I have called you friends"* (John 15:15). Servants receive instructions; friends receive insight. Intimacy shifts the believer from information to revelation, from commands to communion, and from occasional guidance to continual awareness.

The question is not whether God is speaking, but whether the believer understands how He speaks.

The Barriers to Understanding

The crisis for many believers is not the absence of divine communication but the inability to recognise its form. Many expect God to speak dramatically, yet He often speaks quietly. They expect clarity, yet He speaks through process. They expect immediacy, yet He speaks through time.

One primary barrier is unfamiliarity with Scripture. Scripture is the foundational language of God. "*All Scripture is God-breathed*" (2 Timothy 3:16). Without it, the believer lacks the vocabulary to interpret God's voice accurately.

Another barrier is internal noise. The mind becomes crowded with fear, desire, anxiety, and distraction. Yet God often speaks in stillness, as when Elijah encountered Him in a still, small voice (1 Kings 19:12). Noise drowns out subtlety.

Expectations can also limit perception. God does not conform to human preference. "God… spoke in various ways" (Hebrews 1:1). When a believer insists on one method, they become blind to others.

Impatience further weakens sensitivity. Many want God to speak quickly and clearly, yet Scripture reveals that God often speaks through waiting. "*I waited patiently for the Lord*" (Psalm 40:1). Waiting refines perception.

Unbelief closes the heart entirely. "*He did not do many mighty works... because of their unbelief*" (Matthew 13:58). A heart that does not expect God to speak will struggle to recognise His voice.

These barriers, distance from Scripture, internal noise, rigid expectations, impatience, and unbelief, do not silence God, but they distort the believer's ability to hear Him.

The Formation of Spiritual Fluency

The language of intimacy is not mastered by technique but learned through relationship. As the believer walks with God, familiarity grows, and recognition becomes natural.

Scripture forms the foundation of this language. Jesus said, "The words that I speak to you are spirit, and they are life" (John 6:63). Scripture shapes the tone, rhythm, and character of God's voice within the believer.

The Holy Spirit interprets this language. "He will teach you all things" (John 14:26). He illuminates Scripture, clarifies impressions, and guides the believer into truth. Without the Spirit, God's language remains distant; with Him, it becomes clear.

Peace functions as an internal confirmation. *"Let the peace of God rule in your hearts"* (Colossians 3:15).

Peace is not merely emotional; it is directional. It confirms alignment and signals when something is out of place. Conviction refines the heart. Jesus said the Spirit would convict (John 16:8). This is not condemnation but correction. It is God's way of realigning the believer with His truth.

Wisdom provides clarity. *"If any of you lacks wisdom, let him ask of God"* (James 1:5). Wisdom translates divine communication into practical direction.

Silence plays a critical role. *"For God alone my soul waits in silence"* (Psalm 62:5). Silence is not absence; it is formation. In silence, God shapes the believer more than He informs them.

Finally, God speaks through His dealings. *"Whom the Lord loves He disciplines"* (Hebrews 12:6).

His processes, pruning, stretching, refining, are forms of communication. They reveal His priorities and shape the believer's life.

Through these means, the believer moves from hearing God occasionally to understanding Him consistently.

The Call to Understanding

The language of intimacy ultimately poses a question to the believer. Do you recognise the ways God has been speaking to you?

Has He spoken through Scripture, peace, conviction, silence, or the circumstances of your life?

Are you willing to allow God to expand your understanding of His voice?

Intimacy requires openness, humility, and sensitivity.

The deeper question is this: do you desire not only to hear God, but to understand Him?

Final Invitation

God is speaking.

The question is whether you are listening with understanding.

Intimacy is not only nearness; it is communication.

Will you allow the Holy Spirit to teach you God's language?

Part Three

The Cost and Reward of Closeness

CHAPTER NINE

THE ATTENTION OF INTIMACY

The Nature of Attention

Attention is one of the purest expressions of love. It is what the heart treasures, the mind returns to, the eyes linger on, and the soul gravitates towards. Jesus revealed this when He said, "*Where your treasure is, there your heart will be also*" (Matthew 6:21).

Intimacy with God is not sustained by emotion alone; it is sustained by attention, the deliberate turning of the inner gaze towards Him.

Scripture calls this posture "*looking unto Jesus*" (Hebrews 12:2). This is not a momentary glance but a sustained focus. It is the soul choosing to behold God above all else.

Attention reveals value. It reveals desire. It reveals priority. God does not require attention to feel important; He desires it because it is the doorway through which He reveals Himself. "*Draw near to God, and He will draw near to you*" (James 4:8). Attention is the first step towards drawing near.

The question, then, is direct: what holds your attention more than God?

The Crisis of Distraction

The struggle for many believers is not a lack of love for God, but a lack of focused attention. The mind becomes scattered. The heart becomes divided. Life becomes crowded.

Jesus warned that "the cares of this world… choke the word" (Mark 4:19).

Distraction is not harmless; it suffocates spiritual life. A divided heart cannot sustain attention. David prayed, "*Unite my heart to fear Your name*" (Psalm 86:11). Division weakens devotion.

Mental noise compounds the problem. The mind fills with anxiety, responsibility, and a constant internal dialogue. Yet Scripture commands, "*Set your mind on things above*" (Colossians 3:2). A distracted mind cannot perceive God clearly.

Spiritual fatigue further drains attention. Constant stimulation exhausts the soul, leaving little capacity for focus. Jesus' invitation remains: "*Come to Me... and I will give you rest*" (Matthew 11:28). Rest restores attention.

The culture of distraction intensifies this struggle. The world competes for the believer's gaze through constant demands and noise.

Yet God calls the soul into stillness: *"Be still and know that I am God"* (Psalm 46:10).

Inconsistency also weakens attention. Intimacy requires rhythm. Without regular return, focus fades and attention fragments.

The Formation of Focus

Attention is not restored by force but by reorientation, the steady turning of the soul back towards God.

It begins with desire. David wrote, *"One thing I desire... to behold the beauty of the Lord"* (Psalm 27:4). When God becomes the "one thing," attention naturally follows.

Meditation trains attention. *"Meditate on it day and night"* (Joshua 1:8).

Meditation fills the mind with truth, reducing the noise of competing thoughts.

Stillness strengthens focus. "In quietness and confidence shall be your strength" (Isaiah

30:15). Stillness clears the inner space for God to be seen.

Scripture anchors attention. "My eyes are ever toward the Lord" (Psalm 25:15). The Word lifts the gaze and steadies the heart.

Worship gathers attention. "The Father seeks true worshipers" (John 4:23). Worship centres the heart on God with reverence and affection.

Discipline protects attention. "I discipline my body…" (1 Corinthians 9:27). Discipline creates consistency and guards against drift.

Love ultimately sustains attention. Love simplifies the heart, clarifies desire, and keeps the gaze fixed on what matters most.

The Call to Focus

Ultimately, attention confronts the believer with a question.

What has captured your attention when it does not deserve it?

What would your intimacy look like if your focus returned fully to God?

Are you willing to turn your gaze back to Him?

Attention is not automatic; it is chosen.

Final Invitation

God is present.

The question is whether you are looking.

Intimacy is not only nearness, but it is also focus.

Will you give God your attention?

CHAPTER TEN

THE COST OF INTIMACY

The Nature of the Cost

Intimacy with God is beautiful, transformative, and life-giving, yet it is not without cost. The cost is not imposed as payment but required as surrender. Closeness to God demands the release of anything that competes with Him. Jesus made this clear: *"If anyone desires to come after Me, let him deny himself, take up his cross, and follow Me"* (Matthew 16:24).

Intimacy is freely invited, but deeply costly in experience. It requires the surrender of self-will, the yielding of personal agendas, and the willingness to be transformed.

Paul expressed this clearly: *"I count all things loss for the excellence of the knowledge of Christ"* (Philippians 3:8).

This knowledge is not information; it is intimacy. Intimacy requires him to let go of what once defined him.

The question is unavoidable: what does intimacy truly cost?

The Resistance to Sacrifice

Many believers desire intimacy but resist its cost. They seek closeness without surrender, depth without discipline, revelation without obedience, and presence without sacrifice. Yet Scripture consistently reveals that those who walked deeply with God relinquished something to do so.

Abraham left his homeland.
Moses left the palace.

David left comfort.

Paul left status.

Jesus embraced the cross.

Intimacy has always required surrender.

Self-will is often the first barrier. The flesh resists yielding. *"The spirit indeed is willing, but the flesh is weak"* (Matthew 26:41).

Distraction is another obstacle. The world offers constant stimulation, pulling attention away from God. *"Set your mind on things above"* (Colossians 3:2).

Fear of loss prevents surrender. Yet Jesus declared, *"Whoever loses his life for My sake will find it"* (Matthew 16:25). What is surrendered is not lost; it is transformed.

Inconsistency weakens intimacy. Without rhythm, connection fades. The lives of David and Daniel demonstrate that consistency sustains closeness.

Convenience also resists intimacy. The true pursuit of God disrupts comfort and challenges routine. Jesus often withdrew to pray before dawn (Mark 1:35). Intimacy does not accommodate comfort, it reshapes it.

The Formation Through Surrender

The cost of intimacy is not meant to burden the believer, but to free them. Every surrender removes what hinders communion.

Surrender is the beginning. *"Not My will, but Yours be done"* (Luke 22:42). It is the yielding of the lesser for the greater.

Separation follows. God called Abraham to leave what was familiar (Genesis 12:1). Separation is not isolation; it is consecration.

Obedience deepens intimacy. *"If you love Me, keep My commandments"* (John 14:15). Obedience aligns the believer with God's will.

Discipline sustains it. *"I discipline my body..."* (1 Corinthians 9:27). Discipline structures life around God.

Sacrifice expresses devotion. *"I will not offer... that which costs me nothing"* (2 Samuel 24:24). What is valuable is given because God is more valuable.

Purity refines the heart. *"Blessed are the pure in heart..."* (Matthew 5:8). Purity sharpens perception.

Perseverance completes the process. *"Let us run with endurance..."* (Hebrews 12:1). Intimacy is not momentary; it is sustained over time.

The Call to Surrender

The cost of intimacy ultimately confronts the believer with a decision.

What is God asking you to release?

What comfort, distraction, or attachment is competing with your devotion?

Are you willing to surrender what intimacy cannot coexist with?

The question is not whether intimacy is costly; it is. The question is whether you recognise the value it provides.

Final Invitation

Intimacy is not cheap, yet it is worth everything.

God does not force surrender; He invites it.

Intimacy is not only nearness; it is sacrifice.

Will you pay the price to go deeper with Him?

CHAPTER ELEVEN

THE REWARDS OF INTIMACY

The Nature of Inheritance

Intimacy with God is not only costly; it is rewarding. Every sacrifice made in pursuit of God yields a return that far outweighs what was surrendered. Jesus revealed this when He said, "*Your Father who sees in secret will reward you openly*" (Matthew 6:6).

The secret place is not only a place of communion; it is also a place of reward. God does not call the believer into intimacy to diminish them, but to enrich them with Himself.

The question, then, is this: what are the rewards of intimacy?

The rewards are not primarily material, though God may bless materially.

They are not rooted in status, though God may elevate them. The true rewards of intimacy are spiritual, eternal, and transformative.

David captured this when he wrote, *"In Your presence is fullness of joy; at Your right hand are pleasures forevermore"* (Psalm 16:11). Joy is a reward.

Revelation is a reward. Transformation is a reward. God Himself is the reward.

Intimacy produces inheritance. Jesus said, *"I no longer call you servants... but friends"* (John 15:15).

Friendship with God brings access, revelation, authority, and favour.

The question is not whether intimacy is rewarding, but whether the believer recognises what has been given.

The Misunderstanding of Reward

Many believers struggle with intimacy because they misunderstand its rewards.

They expect visible outcomes, ease, comfort, and immediate breakthroughs. Yet the deepest rewards of intimacy are often internal and unfold gradually. When these are overlooked, discouragement follows.

One barrier is the expectation of immediacy. Intimacy often involves a process rather than an instant change.ge Jesus said, *"Every branch that bears fruit He prunes"* (John 15:2). Pruning is preparation, though it may not feel like a reward.

Another misunderstanding is the desire for visibility. Many seek recognition, yet Jesus warned that public approval can be its own shallow reward (Matthew 6:5). Intimacy shapes the inner life before it transforms the outer.

Spiritual blindness also obscures reward. Peace, discernment, stability, and conviction are often overlooked because they are subtle.

Paul prayed that the eyes of understanding would be enlightened (Ephesians 1:18). Without this clarity, the believer misses what God is already giving.

Impatience with timing further distorts perception. *"Though it tarries, wait for it"* (Habakkuk 2:3). God's rewards unfold with purpose, not haste.

Comparison adds another layer of distortion. Jesus said, *"What is that to you? Follow Me"* (John 21:22).

Comparison prevents gratitude, and without gratitude, rewards go unnoticed.

The Substance of the Reward

The rewards of intimacy flow from the nature of God Himself. Intimacy does not merely give what comes from God; it gives God.

Revelation is one of the first rewards. *"To you it has been given to know the mysteries"* (Matthew 13:11). Intimacy opens the believer to understanding that cannot be accessed through intellect alone.

Peace follows. *"My peace I give to you"* (John 14:27). This peace stabilizes the soul beyond circumstance.

Joy strengthens the inner life. *"The joy of the Lord is your strength"* (Nehemiah 8:10). It sustains the believer through difficulty.

Guidance becomes clearer. *"The steps of a good man are ordered by the Lord"* (Psalm 37:23). Intimacy sharpens discernment.

Transformation takes place. *"We... are being transformed"* (2 Corinthians 3:18). Intimacy reshapes the believer into the likeness of Christ.

Protection surrounds life. *"He who dwells... shall abide under the shadow of the Almighty"* (Psalm 91:1).

Favour accompanies nearness. *"You will surround him with favour"* (Psalm 5:12).

Authority flows from a relationship. *"I give you authority"* (Luke 10:19).

Above all, intimacy produces friendship with God. *"The secret of the Lord is with those who fear Him"* (Psalm 25:14).

These are not earned, they are received. They are not demanded, they are given.

The Call to Recognition

The rewards of intimacy confront the believer with a question.

Do you recognise what God has already given you?

Are you valuing the internal work of God as much as external outcomes?

Do you trust God's timing enough to receive what He is forming within you?

Intimacy requires perception as much as pursuit.

Final Invitation

God has already begun to reward your pursuit of Him.

The question is whether you can see it.

Intimacy is not only nearness, but it is also inheritance.

Will you recognise and receive what God is giving you?

CHAPTER TWELVE

INTIMACY AND INTERCESSION

The Nature of Partnership

Intercession is one of the highest expressions of intimacy, where the heart of God and the heart of the believer meet in agreement. It is not merely prayer; it is a partnership.

Scripture reveals this when God says, *"I sought for a man... who would stand in the gap"* (Ezekiel 22:30). Intercession is God searching for a person close enough to Him to carry His burden.

The question is clear: what is the relationship between intimacy and intercession?

Intercession arises from proximity. The closer the believer is to God, the more clearly they perceive His heart.

Jesus said, *"The Son can do nothing of Himself, but what He sees the Father do"* (John

5:19). Intercession flows from seeing, hearing, and sensing God.

God entrusts His burdens to those who are near. *"The secret of the Lord is with those who fear Him"* (Psalm 25:14). Intercession is not given to distance; it is entrusted to intimacy.

The question becomes personal: Is your intimacy deep enough for God to trust you with His burdens?

The Failure of Self-Centred Prayer

The crisis for many believers is not the absence of prayer, but the absence of intercession. Prayer often revolves around personal needs, desires, and concerns. Intercession, however, moves beyond self into the purposes of God. *"Let each of you look not only to his own interests"* (Philippians 2:4).

Self-centred spirituality limits depth. Intercession begins where self-focus ends.

Spiritual dullness also hinders intercession. Many are too distracted to perceive the burdens God bears. Jesus asked, *"Could you not watch with Me one hour?"* (Matthew 26:40). Watching is the posture of intercession.

Fear of responsibility prevents engagement. Intercession carries weight. It requires persistence and endurance.

Unbelief weakens effectiveness. *"The effective, fervent prayer... avails much"* (James 5:16). Without faith, intercession loses force.

Inconsistency limits impact. Intercession thrives on rhythm, not occasional effort.

The Formation of Intercession

Intercession flows naturally from intimacy. It is not a technique, but a response to communion. Compassion is the beginning. Jesus was *"moved with compassion"* (Matthew 9:36). Intercession starts when the heart feels what God feels.

Identification deepens it. Moses stood before God on behalf of Israel (Exodus 32:32). Intercession stands in the place of others.

Alignment sustains it. *"Not My will, but Yours be done"* (Luke 22:42). Intercession reflects God's will, not personal preference.

Authority strengthens it. Abraham interceded boldly (Genesis 18:25). Authority flows from intimacy.

Persistence carries it forward. Elijah prayed repeatedly until the answer came (1 Kings 18:43–44). Intercession does not withdraw.

Burden-bearing defines it. *"Bear one another's burdens"* (Galatians 6:2). Intercession carries weight with purpose.

Spiritual sensitivity completes it. *"The Spirit... intercedes for us"* (Romans 8:26). True intercession is Spirit-led and Spirit-sustained.

The Call to Partnership

Intercession ultimately confronts the believer with a question.

Do you feel what God is asking you to carry?

Are you willing to pray for what He desires, not only what you desire?

Will you remain with Him in prayer, even when it is costly?

Intercession is not an obligation; it is an invitation.

Final Invitation

God is still seeking those who will stand in the gap.

The question is whether you will stand with Him.

Intimacy is not only nearness, but it is also partnership.

Will you become one who carries the heart of God?

CHAPTER THIRTEEN

WALKING WITH THE HOLY SPIRIT

The Nature of Companionship

Walking with the Holy Spirit is one of the greatest privileges of the believer's life. He is not a distant force, an abstract presence, or a theological idea. He is a Person, the Spirit of God, given to dwell within, guide, teach, strengthen, and reveal Christ.

Jesus promised, *"I will pray the Father, and He will give you another Helper, that He may abide with you forever"* (John 14:16). The Spirit is not temporary; He is permanent.

He is not occasional; He is constant. He is not external; He is within.

The question, then, is simple: what does it mean to walk with the Holy Spirit?

Walking implies movement, rhythm, agreement, and companionship. Scripture says, *"If we live in the Spirit, let us also walk in the Spirit"* (Galatians 5:25). Living in the Spirit is the reality of salvation; walking in the Spirit is the expression of intimacy.

The Spirit leads, but He does not force. He guides, but He does not compel. He invites, but He does not override the will. Walking with Him requires sensitivity, attention, and willingness to follow.

The deeper question is this: are you walking with the Spirit, or merely aware of Him?

The Fractures of Disconnection

The challenge for many believers is not the absence of the Holy Spirit, but the absence of active companionship with Him.

They acknowledge His presence but do not cultivate a relationship. They desire His power but resist His leadership.

They want His gifts but neglect His voice. Scripture warns, *"Do not grieve the Holy Spirit"* (Ephesians 4:30). Grief reflects relational neglect, not distance. One of the primary fractures is independence. Many attempt to navigate life by personal strength and reasoning. Yet Scripture instructs, "Lean not on your own understanding" (Proverbs 3:5). Independence weakens reliance and disrupts intimacy.

Insensitivity is another barrier. The Spirit speaks quietly, through conviction, prompting, and inner witness. Yet distraction dulls perception, so hearing must be cultivated. Resistance also interrupts companionship. The Spirit leads towards truth, holiness, and transformation, while the flesh resists that movement. This tension weakens responsiveness.

Inconsistency further disrupts the walk. Companionship requires rhythm, yet many engage with the Spirit sporadically. Intimacy, however, grows through constancy.

Misunderstanding adds another layer. Many reduce the Spirit to power, experience, or event, rather than relating to Him as a Person. But Jesus described Him as Helper, Teacher, Guide, and Comforter. Without this understanding, the relationship remains shallow. These fractures create believers who possess the Spirit but do not walk with Him.

The Formation of the Walk

Walking with the Holy Spirit is not complex; it is relational. It is the daily practice of awareness, response, and alignment. It begins with awareness. *"Do you not know that you are the temple... and that the Spirit of God dwells in you?"* (1 Corinthians 3:16). Awareness shifts the believer from living for God to living with God.

Yielding follows awareness. *"As many as are led by the Spirit of God, these are sons of God"* (Romans 8:14). Leading requires yielding, and yielding requires trust.

Obedience deepens the relationship. The Spirit does not speak merely to inform, but to transform. Obedience strengthens sensitivity and reinforces intimacy.

Sensitivity develops through attention. The believer learns to discern the Spirit's movements, His promptings, warnings, and guidance. This awareness becomes clearer over time.

Fellowship sustains the relationship. Scripture speaks of *"the fellowship of the Holy Spirit"* (2 Corinthians 13:14). Fellowship involves communion, listening, and response. It is relational, not mechanical.

Dependence strengthens the walk. Jesus said, *"Without Me you can do nothing"* (John 15:5). Dependence is not weakness; it is alignment with the source of life.

Holiness reflects the nature of the Spirit. *"Walk in the Spirit, and you shall not fulfil the lust of the flesh"* (Galatians 5:16). Holiness is not restriction; it is harmony with His nature.

Through these movements, the believer shifts from awareness of the Spirit to companionship with Him.

The Call to Walk

Walking with the Spirit ultimately confronts the believer with a decision. Are you aware of His presence within you? Are you willing to yield your will to His leading?

Will you allow Him to guide your steps, shape your thoughts, and govern your decisions?

Walking requires consistency. It requires attentiveness. It requires surrender.

The Spirit is present, but the relationship must be cultivated.

Final Invitation

The Holy Spirit is not distant. He is near. He is present. He is within.

The question is not whether He is with you, but whether you are walking with Him.

Intimacy is not only nearness, but it is also companionship.

Will you walk with the Holy Spirit daily?

Part Four

The Maturity Dimension of Intimacy

CHAPTER FOURTEEN

THE SECRET PLACE LIFESTYLE

The Nature of Habitation

The secret place is not a moment, an event, or a spiritual activity. It is a lifestyle, a continual dwelling in the presence of God. Jesus revealed this when He said, "When you pray, go into your room… and pray to your Father who is in the secret place" (Matthew 6:6). The secret place is not where God occasionally visits; it is where He dwells. It is the inner sanctuary of communion, the hidden space where the believer meets God in quietness and sincerity.

To live in the secret place is defined not by physical location but by spiritual posture. David expressed this when he wrote, *"He who dwells in the secret place of the Most High shall abide under the shadow of the Almighty"* (Psalm 91:1).

Dwelling is not visiting, and abiding is not occasional. The secret place is a life anchored in the awareness of God's presence.

God calls the believer into the secret place because intimacy requires privacy. In hiddenness, clarity is formed, identity is affirmed, and the soul is restored. Jesus Himself modelled this life, regularly withdrawing to commune with the Father. The secret place, therefore, is not an accessory to spiritual life; it is its foundation.

The question that confronts the believer is simple yet searching: Are you living in the secret place, or merely visiting it?

The Fractures of Inconsistency

The difficulty for many believers is not the absence of prayer, but the absence of dwelling. Their engagement with God becomes occasional, emotional, or circumstantial, rather than consistent and rooted.

Inconsistency is one of the primary fractures. Many approach God only when they feel inclined or in need. Yet intimacy is not sustained by emotion but by rhythm. The life of devotion requires regular return, not sporadic engagement.

Distraction further weakens the ability to dwell. The demands of life scatter attention and divide the heart. Jesus' words to Martha reveal the danger of a life overwhelmed by many concerns, in which the essential is overshadowed by the urgent. Without focus, the secret place becomes neglected.

Superficiality also limits intimacy. It is possible to pray without truly engaging, to speak without listening, and to enter without remaining.

Yet Jesus calls the believer not merely to approach Him, but to abide in Him. Depth requires time, attentiveness, and intentional presence.

Spiritual dryness often follows neglect of the secret place. When the inner life is severed from communion with God, it loses vitality. Scripture presents God's presence as a well from which the soul draws life. Without that well, the spirit grows weary.

Many avoid the secret place because of the silence. Silence exposes the heart's inner condition, which can be uncomfortable. Yet it is often in that quietness that God speaks most clearly. Avoiding silence is, in effect, avoiding intimacy.

These fractures produce believers who love God yet do not dwell with Him.

The Formation of Habitation

The secret place lifestyle is not formed instantly; it is cultivated intentionally. It is the shaping of life around the presence of God until that presence becomes the believer's natural environment.

It begins with desire. When the heart longs for God above all else, it naturally turns towards Him. Desire draws the soul into communion and sustains its pursuit.

Withdrawal creates the necessary space for intimacy. This is not withdrawal from responsibility, but from noise. It is the deliberate choice to step away from distraction to attend to God.

Stillness quiets the inner life and allows awareness to deepen. In stillness, the believer becomes attentive, no longer driven by urgency but settled in the presence.

Meditation anchors the mind in truth. By filling the inner life with Scripture, the believer aligns with the voice and nature of God.

Abiding sustains the relationship. It is the continual choice to remain in God, not only in moments of prayer but throughout the rhythms of daily life.

Secrecy protects the authenticity of devotion. What is cultivated in hiddenness is not performed for others but offered sincerely to God.

Constancy establishes the lifestyle. Through consistent return, the secret place shifts from an activity to a dwelling.

Through these movements, intimacy becomes habitation.

The Call to Dwell

The secret place ultimately confronts the believer with a decision.

Has your life been built around the presence of God, or is His presence something you visit only when needed? What must be removed, rearranged, or surrendered for you to dwell consistently? Are you willing to allow God's presence to become your home rather than your refuge? The invitation is not merely to visit God but to live with Him.

Final Invitation

God is present in the secret place, waiting not for occasional attention, but for continual dwelling. The question is not whether He is there, but whether you will remain. Intimacy is not only nearness, but it is also habitation. **Will you dwell in His presence?**

CHAPTER FIFTEEN

WHEN INTIMACY BECOMES PRAYER

The Nature of Overflow

There comes a point in the believer's journey when prayer is no longer an activity, discipline, or obligation. It becomes the natural overflow of intimacy. It becomes instinctive, continuous, and deeply relational, the language of a heart shaped by nearness to God.

Jesus said, "*Your Father knows what you need before you ask Him*" (Matthew 6:8). This shows that, in its highest form, prayer is not about informing God but about communing with Him. It is the soul leaning into the presence of the One it loves.

When intimacy matures, prayer shifts from effort to expression. The believer no longer prays from a distance, but from union. God is no longer approached as distant, but known as Father. Scripture describes this reality as the Spirit within crying, *"Abba, Father"* (Galatians 4:6). This cry is not taught; it is formed within the heart.

Prayer, in this dimension, is no longer external; it is internal, continuous, and alive.

The Transformation of Prayer

As intimacy deepens, the nature of prayer is transformed.

Prayer is no longer primarily a request; it becomes a response. The believer begins to echo what God is already speaking, aligning their voice with His will. Jesus demonstrated this when He said that He acted only in accordance with what He perceived from the Father.

Prayer becomes participation rather than petition. It is the act of seeing what God is doing and agreeing with it, of hearing His voice and yielding to it, and of aligning the will with divine purpose.

In this place, presence becomes central. The priority of prayer shifts from outcomes to communion. Moses expressed this when he refused to move forward without God's presence. The presence itself becomes the pursuit.

Prayer is no longer measured by length, eloquence, or intensity, but by the depth of communion.

The Depth of Communion

This dimension of prayer is marked by stillness. Stillness is not inactivity, but awareness.

It is the quieting of the inner life so that the spirit can perceive God without interference.

In stillness, the believer begins to listen more than speak, to receive more than request, and to behold rather than strive. God’s voice becomes clearer, not because He speaks louder, but because the soul becomes quieter.

As intimacy deepens, the believer's desires are reshaped. Prayer is no longer driven by personal preference, but by the Spirit. Scripture reveals that the Spirit intercedes within the believer, forming the burden, shaping the cry, and directing the prayer.

Prayer moves beyond personal agenda into divine alignment. It becomes the place where the believer's heart is moulded into the likeness of Christ.

The Lifestyle of Prayer

When intimacy becomes prayer, it becomes continual. What once felt like discipline becomes natural.

Prayer becomes the posture of the heart, the rhythm of the inner life, and the atmosphere in which the believer lives.

The presence of God permeates every moment, shaping decisions, conversations, and responses. Prayer is no longer confined to specific times; it becomes the undercurrent of existence.

In this place, prayer becomes transformative. As the believer remains in communion, they are gradually changed. Their thoughts are renewed, their desires refined, and their identity strengthened.

Boldness also emerges. This boldness is not arrogance but confidence rooted in a relationship.

The believer approaches God with assurance, not as a stranger, but as one who is known and loved.

Life itself becomes an altar. Every aspect of the believer's existence becomes an offering, thoughts, decisions, actions, and surrender. Prayer is no longer something they do; it is who they are.

The Call to Communion

The progression of intimacy leads to a defining realisation: prayer is not ultimately about answers, but about God Himself.

The believer discovers that the greatest reward of prayer is not what is received, but who is encountered. The pursuit of God replaces the pursuit of outcomes.

The question, then, becomes deeply personal. Are you willing to allow your life to be shaped into continual communion? Are you willing to move beyond structured moments of prayer into a life that remains connected to God at all times?

Final Invitation

The highest expression of intimacy is a life that prays without ceasing, living in constant communion.

The reward of prayer is God Himself.

Intimacy is not only nearness, but it is also prayer.

Will you allow your life to become a continual expression of communion with Him?

CHAPTER SIXTEEN

THE WATCHMAN'S INTIMACY

The Nature of Vigilance

There is a dimension of intimacy that not only draws the believer into communion with God but also positions them as a watchman, one who stands between heaven and earth, perceiving what others do not see, hearing what others do not hear, and carrying the burden of God's heart with clarity and sobriety. The watchman is not a title; it is a posture formed through intimacy matured into vigilance. Scripture reveals this calling when God declares, *"I have set watchmen on your walls… they shall never hold their peace, day or night"* (Isaiah 62:6). Watchmen are not appointed by human systems; they are raised in the presence of God. Their authority is not derived from position but from proximity.

When intimacy matures into watchfulness, the believer becomes alert in the Spirit. They develop sensitivity to God's movements and awareness of the enemy's strategies. They discern seasons, shifts, and atmospheres. They intercede not as a duty but as a calling rooted in relationship.

The watchman hears so they may speak accurately, sees so they may stand faithfully, and senses so they may pray effectively. Their life becomes a continual posture of listening.

The Sensitivity of the Watchman

The watchman's intimacy is marked by heightened sensitivity to God's voice. They do not depend on dramatic manifestations; they respond to subtle movements. They understand that God often speaks in whispers, and they have trained their hearts to recognise that whisper.

Elijah's encounter with God reveals this pattern. God was not in the wind, the earthquake, or the fire, but in a still, small voice. The watchman learns to value that quiet voice above external signs.

This sensitivity produces spiritual alertness. Jesus warned, *"Watch and pray"* (Matthew 26:41). Watchfulness is not fear-driven; it is discernment. It is the ability to recognise when the atmosphere shifts, when the heart drifts, or when danger approaches.

Because of intimacy, the watchman is not spiritually asleep. They remain aware, attentive, and responsive.

The Burden of Partnership

The watchman's intimacy is also marked by burden. God shares His heart with those who are near Him, and His heart carries weight.

This burden is not heaviness for its own sake; it is the privilege of partnership. Jeremiah described this burden as a fire within. It is the inward urgency that compels response.

The watchman feels what God feels: His desire for restoration, His grief over sin, and His longing for repentance.

In this dimension, prayer becomes strategic. It is no longer general or reactive but precise, informed by spiritual perception. The watchman prays with insight, aligning with what is revealed through intimacy. Aware of spiritual realities, they are not easily caught off guard.

They stand in the gap, resisting darkness and aligning circumstances with God's will. In this dimension, prayer becomes strategic. It is no longer general or reactive but precise, informed by spiritual perception.

The watchman prays with insight, aligning with what is revealed through intimacy. Aware of spiritual realities, they are not easily caught off guard. They stand in the gap, resisting darkness and aligning circumstances with God's will.

The Responsibility of Obedience

Watchfulness entails responsibility. When God speaks, the watchman responds. When God warns, they act. When God burdens them, they pray.

This obedience is not optional; it is integral to the watchman's role. Scripture reveals that withholding a warning carries a consequence. The watchman's responsiveness becomes protection for others. Their obedience becomes a covering.

Purity is essential in this dimension. A divided heart, a distracted mind, or a compromised life weakens perception. Jesus said, "Blessed are the pure in heart, for they shall see God" (Matthew 5:8). Purity sharpens vision and safeguards discernment.

Endurance also defines the watchman. They do not abandon their post. They remain steadfast, sustained not by human effort but by grace flowing from intimacy.

The Call to Stand

The watchman ultimately stands on behalf of others. They become guardians in the spirit, watching over families, communities, and generations.

Their lives carry heaven's perspective into earthly situations.

This calling is not visible or celebrated. It is often hidden and misunderstood. Yet it is deeply valued by God, who continues to seek those willing to stand in the gap.

The question, therefore, becomes deeply personal. Are you willing to remain alert, to carry what God entrusts to you, and to respond with obedience? Are you willing to stand, even when unseen, and to pray with consistency and clarity?

Final Invitation

Watchfulness is not a burden; it is a privilege. It is an honour to be entrusted with God's heart and to participate in His purposes. Intimacy is not only nearness, but it is also vigilance.

Will you stand as a watchman before God?

CHAPTER SEVENTEEN

THE JOURNEY INTO ONENESS

The Nature of Union

What does it mean to become one with God, not in metaphor, but in lived spiritual reality? What does it mean for the believer's inner life to be so aligned, surrendered, and filled with God's presence that separation dissolves and union becomes the atmosphere of existence?

Jesus revealed this possibility in His prayer: *"That they all may be one... as You, Father, are in Me, and I in You"* (John 17:21). This is not symbolic language. It is an invitation to union.

Oneness is not merely closeness; it is participation. It is not simply walking with God, but living from Him. '

Scripture affirms this reality: *"He who is joined to the Lord is one spirit with Him"* (1 Corinthians 6:17).

The question is not whether oneness is possible, but whether the believer will yield to the journey that leads into it.

The Fractures That Prevent Union

The primary barrier to oneness is not distance from God, but division within the heart. Many believers live fragmented lives, pulled by competing desires and shaped by distractions that weaken spiritual sensitivity.

A divided heart cannot sustain union.

Inner conflict is one of the earliest fractures. The believer desires God yet resists surrender. The tension between flesh and spirit breeds instability, preventing rest in God.

Inconsistency further disrupts the union. Oneness requires abiding, yet many vacillate between closeness and distance. Abiding is not occasional; it is continual.

Misaligned desires also hinder union. When the heart is divided between God and lesser attachments, intimacy weakens. Scripture calls for a purified heart, wholly directed towards God.

Noise adds another layer of resistance. The inner life becomes crowded, making it difficult to perceive God's voice. Yet God often speaks quietly, requiring stillness to be heard.

Fear of surrender remains one of the deepest obstacles. Oneness requires yielding control, and many resist because they fear loss. Yet the paradox of intimacy is that what is surrendered is ultimately found.

These fractures prevent the believer from entering the fullness of union.

The Formation of Oneness

The journey into oneness is not achieved through striving, but through surrender. It is the gradual yielding of the inner life until union becomes natural.

It begins with surrender. The believer releases control, allowing God to shape their will, desires, and identity. Oneness begins where self is no longer central.

The heart must be unified. A focused, undivided heart becomes the foundation of union. When the inner life is aligned, intimacy deepens.

Stillness creates the environment for union. In quietness, distractions that fragment awareness are set aside, and the presence of God becomes clearer.

Beholding transforms the believer. As they fix their attention on God, they are changed into His likeness. This transformation leads to union.

Awareness shifts from external pursuit to internal recognition. God is no longer perceived as distant but known as present within.

Rest becomes the atmosphere of oneness. The soul ceases striving and settles into God as its dwelling place.

Love ultimately binds the relationship. Love unites, merges, and sustains the connection between the believer and God.

Through these movements, the believer moves from seeking God to living in Him.

The Call to Union

Oneness ultimately confronts the believer with a question.

Are you willing to surrender what cannot enter into union? Are you prepared to let go of distractions, fear, and divided desires? Are you willing to abide fully, not occasionally but continually? Oneness is not for the casual seeker but for the surrendered life. It requires willingness, not perfection, but yielding.

Final Invitation

God invites the believer into union, but He does not force it.

The invitation remains open. Intimacy is not only nearness, but it is also oneness.

Will you allow your life to become one with Him?

CONCLUSION

THE FINAL CALL TO INTIMACY

Intimacy is not a destination reached once and celebrated forever. It is a life continually yielded to the presence of God. It is the daily decision to turn the heart toward Him, to quiet the noise, to surrender the will, and to dwell in the place where His presence becomes the atmosphere of existence.

Every chapter in this book has been an invitation—each one a doorway, each one a quiet call into deeper nearness. But the true journey does not end with reading. It begins with living.

God is not far. He has never been far. He is the God who draws near, the God who calls, the God who waits, the God who desires to make His home within the surrendered heart. The mystery of intimacy is not that God hides Himself, but that the human soul must learn to see. The mystery of nearness is not that God withdraws, but that the believer must learn to remain. The mystery of oneness is not that God withholds union, but that the heart must yield to the love that transforms.

If something within you has been stirred, do not ignore it. If you have sensed hunger, guard it. If you have heard His whisper, honour it. If you have felt the weight of His presence, remain there.

Hunger opens the door.

Stillness reveals what is hidden.

Surrender leads to union.

Love sustains the journey.

Let this book not become a memory, but a beginning. Let it not remain a moment, but become a movement within your life. And may the God who called you into intimacy lead you into depths you have not yet imagined. The journey continues. The invitation remains.

Come closer.

AFTERWORD

THE WHISPER BEHIND THE PAGES

Every word in this book was written under the quiet weight of God's presence. There were moments when the writing felt like prayer, moments when the sentences felt like surrender, and moments when the pages carried more than language; they carried encounter.

These chapters were not written from mastery, but from a journey. They were written by one learning to walk with God, to hear Him, to trust Him, and to yield to Him. If these pages awakened something within you, it is because the Holy Spirit breathed upon them. If they stirred hunger, it is because He is drawing you. If they brought clarity, it is because He is teaching you. If they brought conviction, it is because He is aligning you. If they brought peace, it is because He is near.

My prayer is that long after this book is closed, the whisper of God will remain. That the hunger will deepen. That the stillness will grow. That awareness will sharpen. That surrender will become joy.

And that intimacy will become your dwelling place.

ABOUT THE AUTHOR

Oluwakemi T. Amuda is a career diplomat, author, and writer whose work centres on the pursuit of God, the formation of the inner life, and the transformation that flows from intimacy with the Holy Spirit.

Her writing is marked by depth, clarity, and reverence for God's presence. She writes with the desire that every reader will encounter God personally and discover the beauty of a life fully surrendered to Him.

Her passion is to guide believers beyond routine into relationship, beyond activity into encounter, and beyond nearness into oneness. Through her writing, teaching, and ministry, she invites readers into a deeper walk with God, one marked by stillness, surrender, and abiding presence.

She is a mother, a leader, a diplomat, and a vessel committed to carrying the fragrance of God into every sphere of influence. Her life's desire is simple: to know God deeply and to help others do the same.

A NOTE TO THE READER

If this book has stirred something within you, pause and acknowledge God. That stirring is not human; it is divine. It is the evidence of His drawing. Do not rush past it. Do not silence it. Let it lead you.

Return to these pages when your heart feels distant. Read slowly. Pray deeply. Sit quietly. Allow the Holy Spirit to breathe upon the words again. Intimacy is not learned in a moment. It is cultivated over a lifetime.

And remember this:

God desires you.
God delights in you.
God calls you by name.
And He is nearer than your breath.

SCRIPTURE CREDITS

All Scripture quotations are taken from the Holy Bible.

CLOSING PRAYER

THE SEAL OF INTIMACY

Father, I come before You with a heart awakened, a spirit stirred, and a soul that has tasted the sweetness of Your nearness. I thank You for every whisper, every revelation, every moment of stillness, and every gentle drawing that has led me into deeper awareness of You.

I acknowledge that intimacy is not something I can create. It is something You invite me into. And so I respond with humility, with surrender, and with desire.

Unite my heart to fear Your name. Quiet every voice that competes with Yours. Silence every distraction that pulls me away from Your presence. Heal every fracture within me that resists surrender. Purify every desire that does not lead me into You.

Holy Spirit, teach me to abide. Teach me to remain. Teach me to dwell. Let intimacy become my lifestyle, not my moment. Let nearness become my home, not my visit. Let Your presence become the atmosphere of my inner life.

Jesus, draw me into the oneness You prayed for. Make me one with You in will, in love, in purpose, and in spirit. Let my life be hidden in Yours. Let my identity be rooted in Yours. Let my steps follow Yours. Let my voice echo Yours.

Father, I yield every part of me that cannot enter oneness. I lay down fear. I lay down striving. I lay down self-will. I lay down the distraction. I choose stillness. I choose to surrender. I choose You.

Let this journey not end here. Let it deepen. Let it transform me from the inside out. Let every truth take root, bear fruit, and shape my life into a testimony of intimacy with You.

And now I ask for one thing:

Draw me closer.

Closer than I have been.

Closer than I understand.

Closer until nearness becomes union,

and union becomes oneness, and oneness

becomes my life. In Jesus' name, Amen.

www.ingramcontent.com/pod-product-compliance
Lightning Source LLC
LaVergne TN
LVHW090611110826
845146LV00001B/348

* 9 7 9 8 9 9 5 6 4 5 8 8 7 *